THIS BOOK BELONGS TO:

_____

LIFE SAVERS NAME HERE

I SAVE LIVES
&
SO CAN YOU!

A CHILDREN'S GUIDE IN HELPING DURING CPR

WRITTEN BY E.M.T. JAVI

GENERAL DISCLAIMER

Published by

CGMOVEMENTS LLC

First Printing Edition 2023 in United States

Copyright © 2023 E.M.T Javi

Dedicated to my Mother, family, and friends. Thanks to everyone who has ever helped teach someone how to save a life!

-Love, Javi-

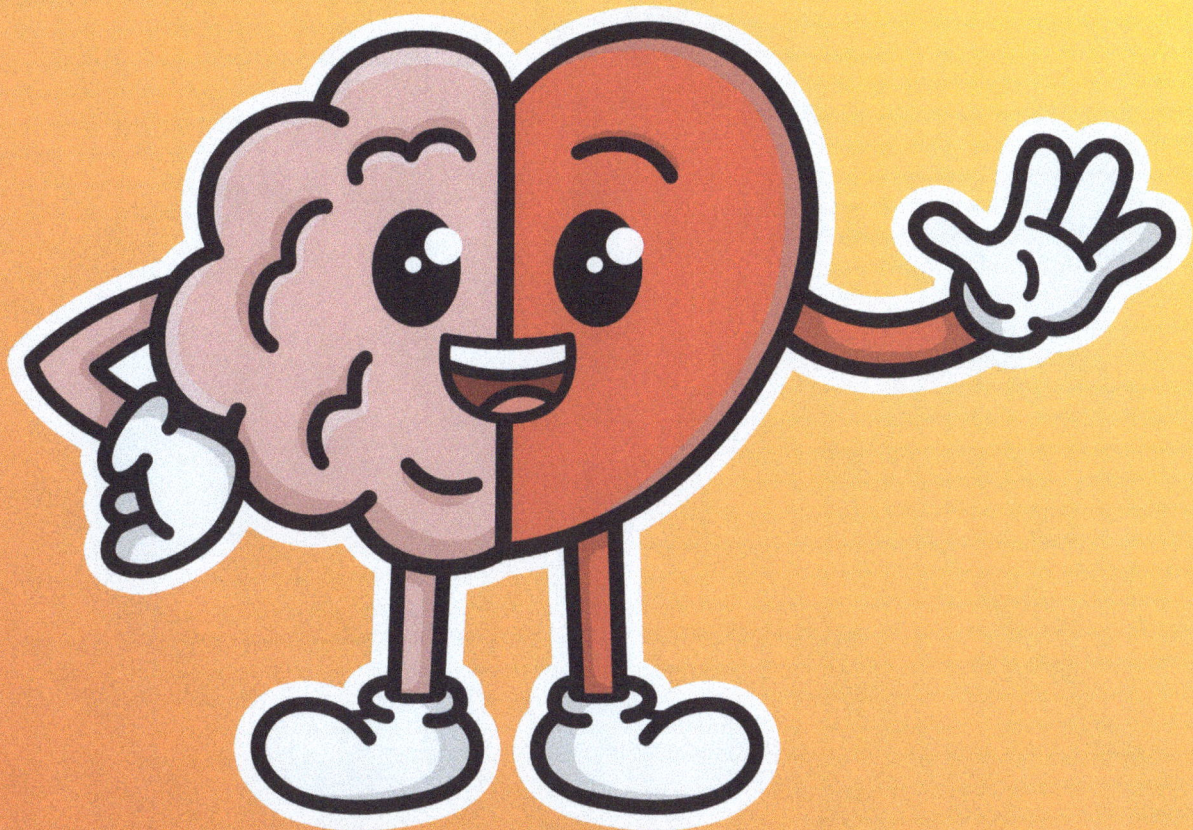

HI, MY NAME IS COR-B
AND MY, OH MY,
DO I HAVE A STORY FOR
YOU.

I WANT YOU ALL TO LISTEN CAREFULLY BECAUSE ALL OF THIS IS TRUE.

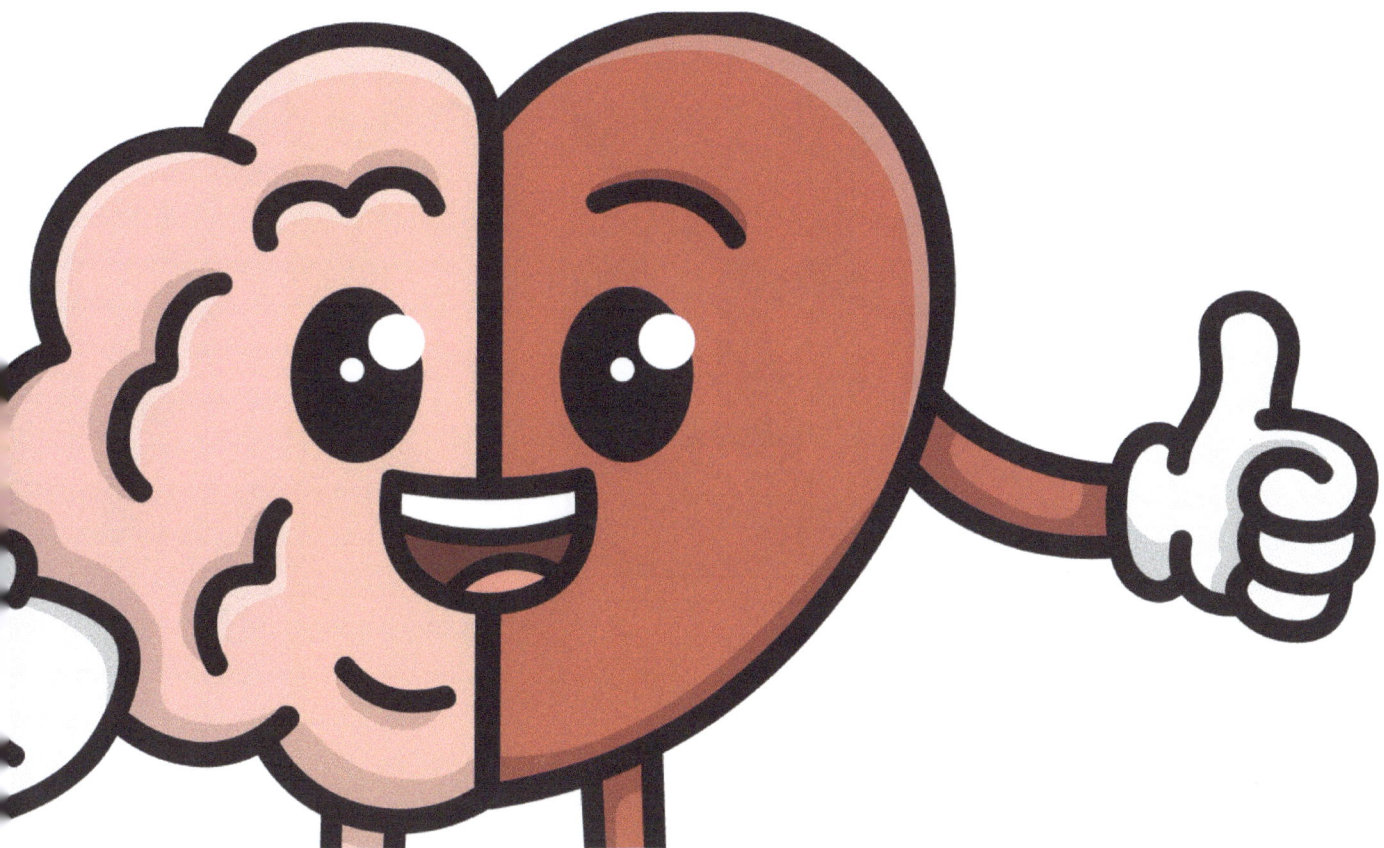

TODAY WE LEARN THE TALE OF HOW TO SAVE A BRAIN AND HEART.

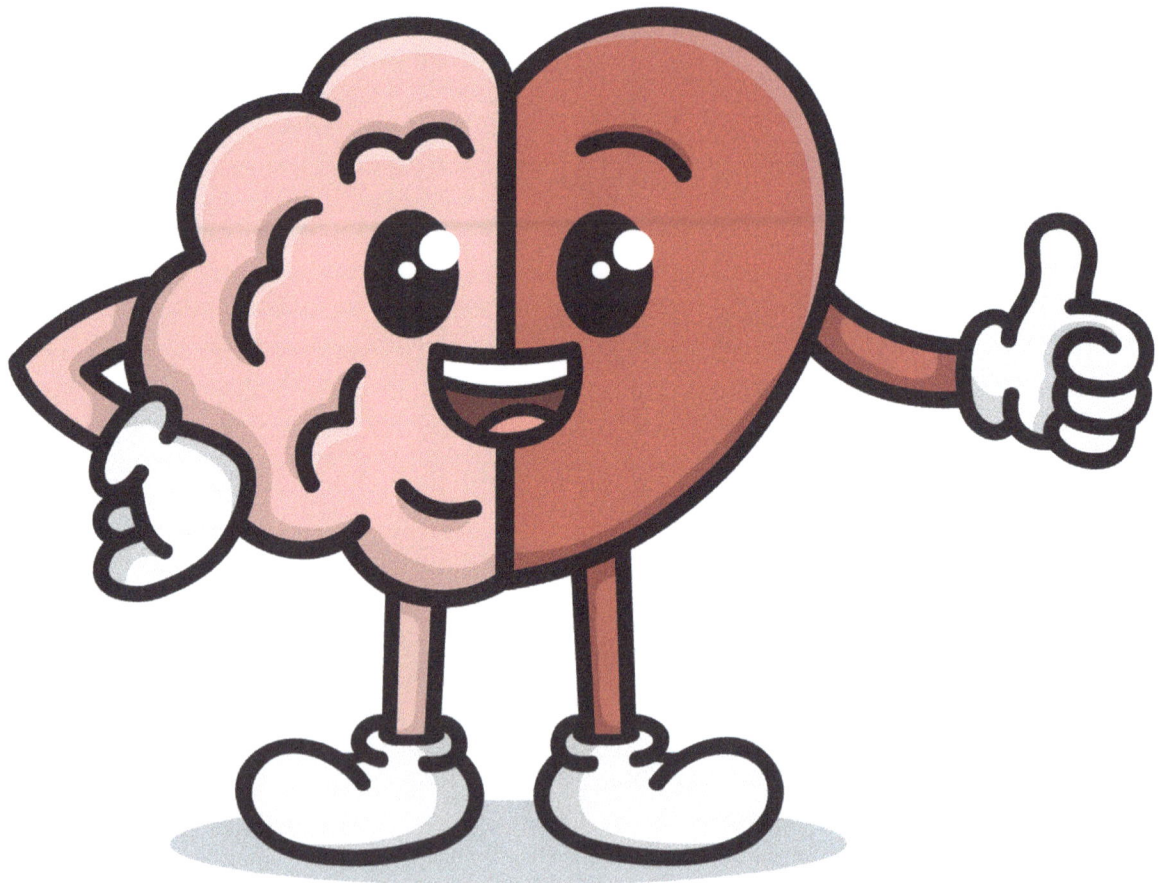

SO LET YOUR MIND SOAK IT IN.
TURN THE PAGE.
WE ARE READY TO START.

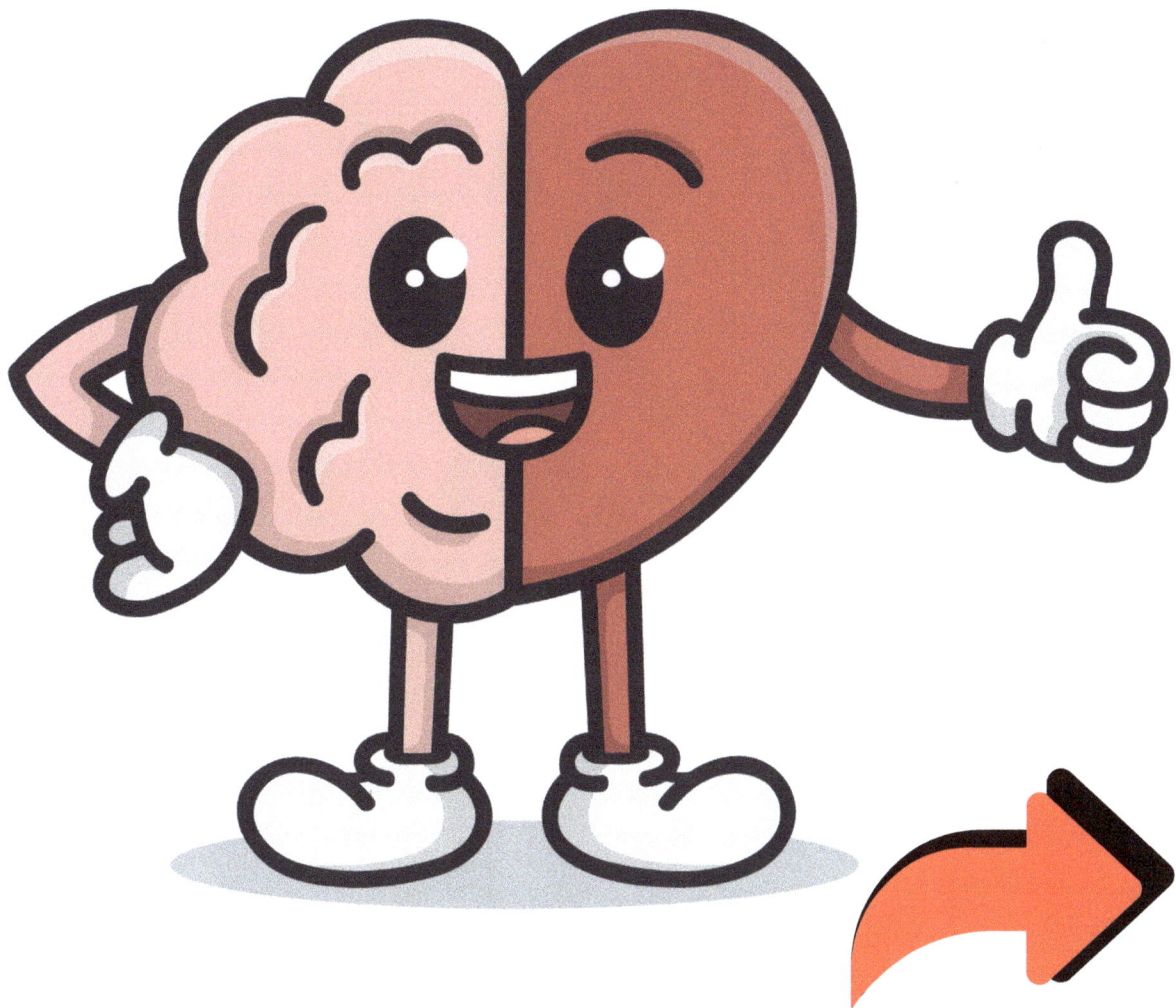

WE HAVE NUMBERS.
WE HAVE NUMBERS.
WE HAVE NUMBERS TO
MEMORIZE.

TAKE A BREATH,
JUST STAY CALM.
WE GOT THINGS
TO RECOGNIZE.

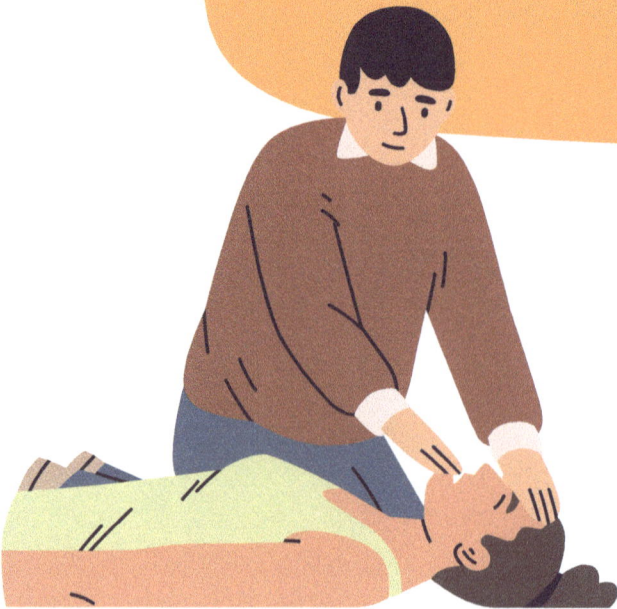

YELL FOR HELP FROM AN ADULT AND SAY, "CPR IS EASY JUST REMEMBER 30 AND 2."

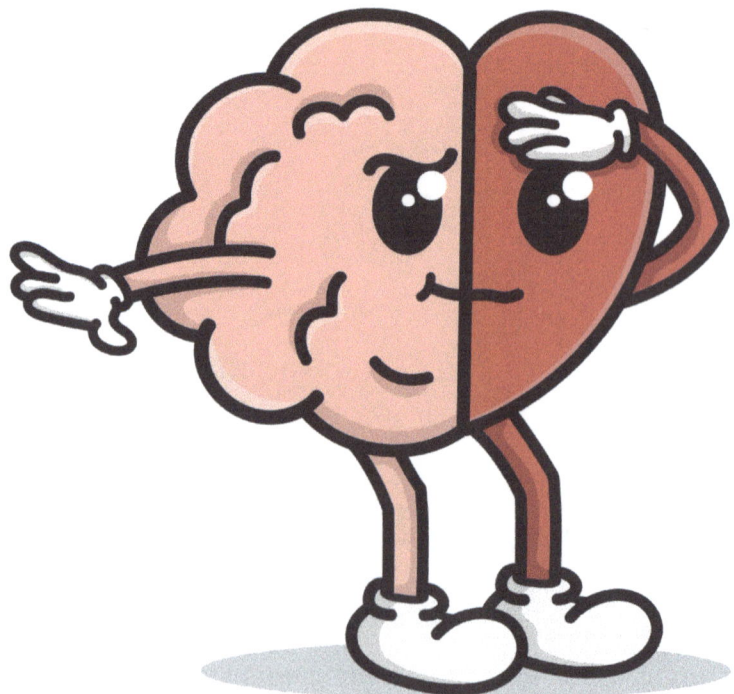

BE AWARE OF YOUR SURROUNDINGS AND STEER CLEAR OF ALL DANGER.

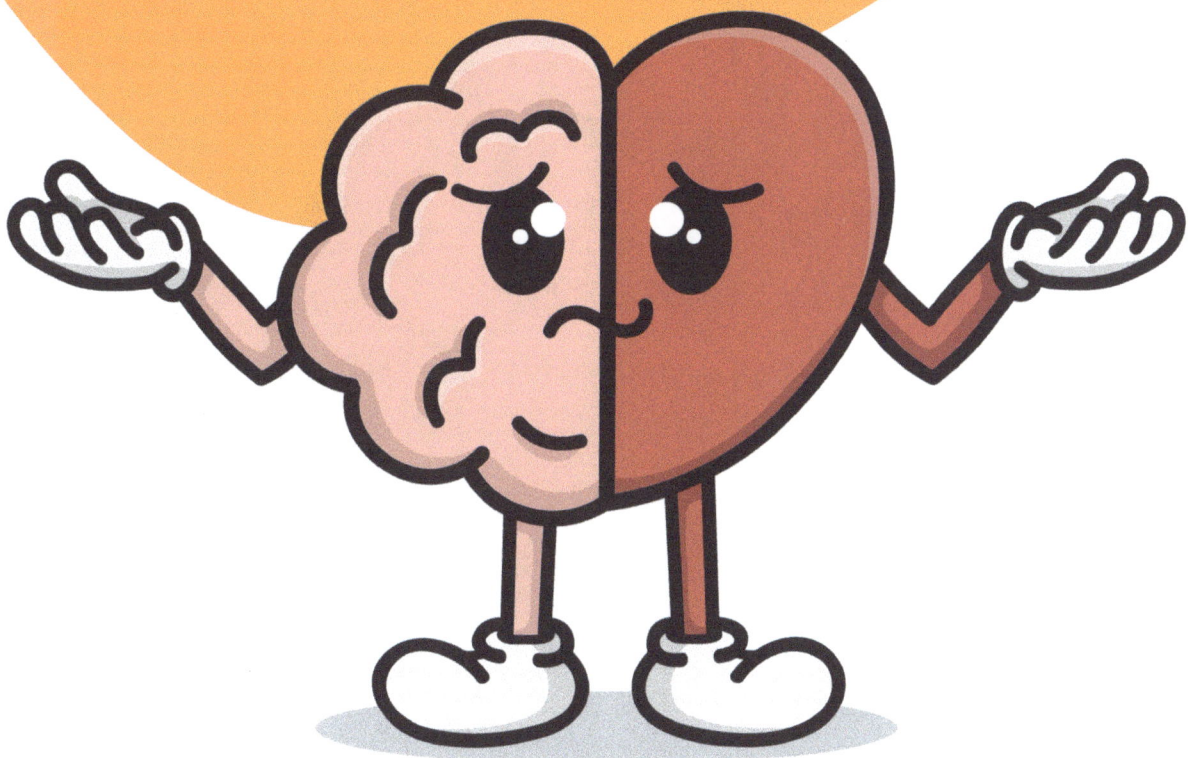

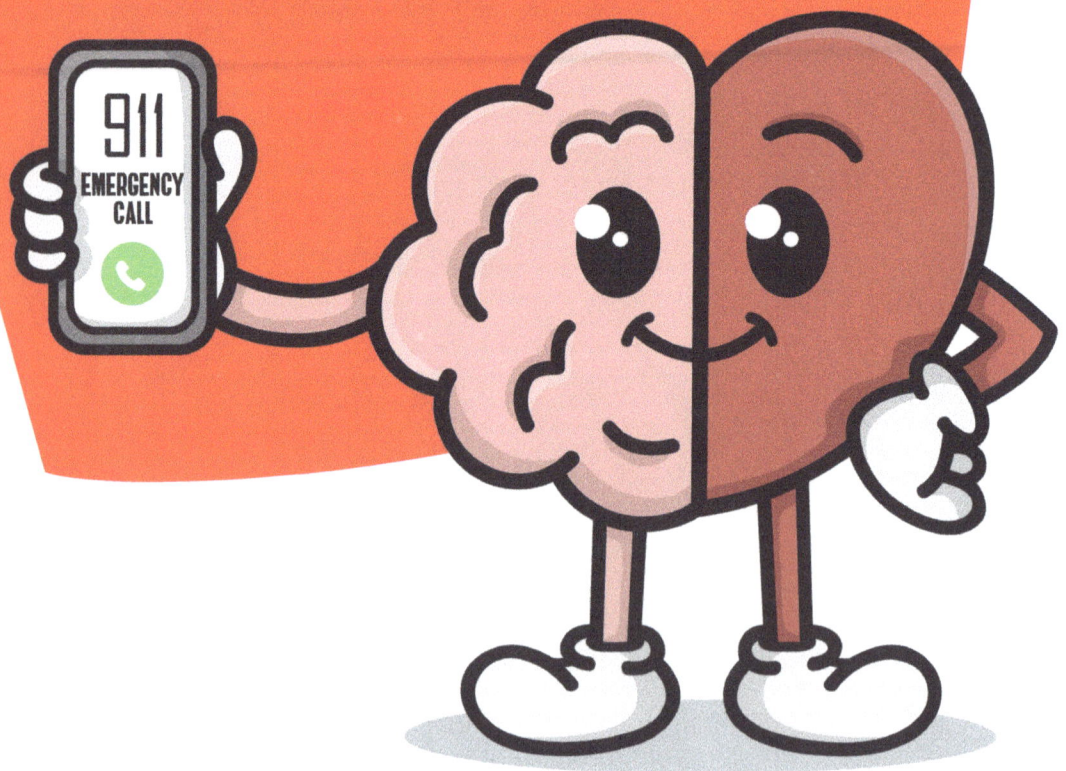

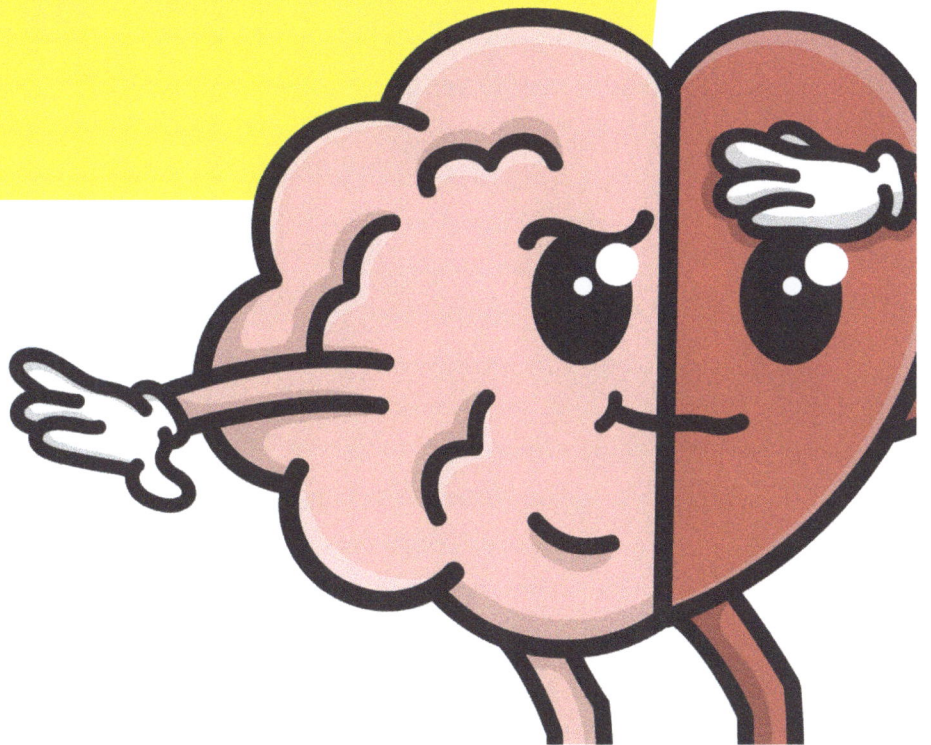

WHILE THIS PERSON IS LYING THERE, MAKE SURE IT'S A STURDY FLAT SURFACE.

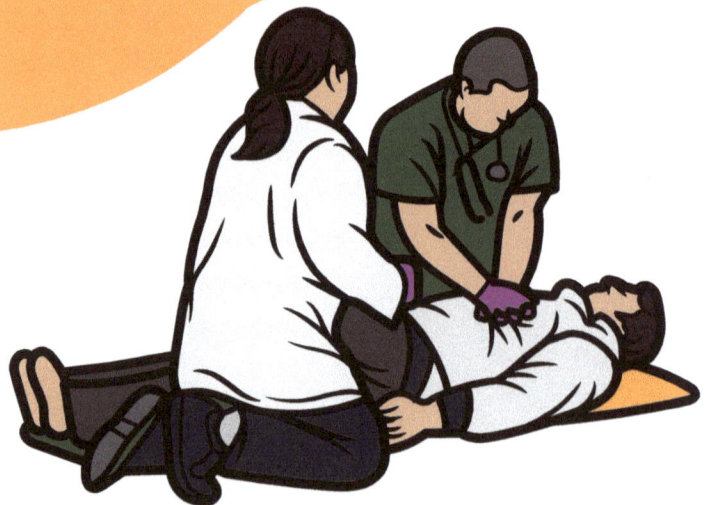

YOU CAN EVEN
SING A SONG CAUSE
WE ARE TRYING TO
STAY ALIVE.

WHAT'S NEXT?
WHAT'S NEXT?
NO MATTER
WHERE WE
ARE.

WHAT WE ARE LOOKING FOR SHOULD NOT BE TOO FAR.

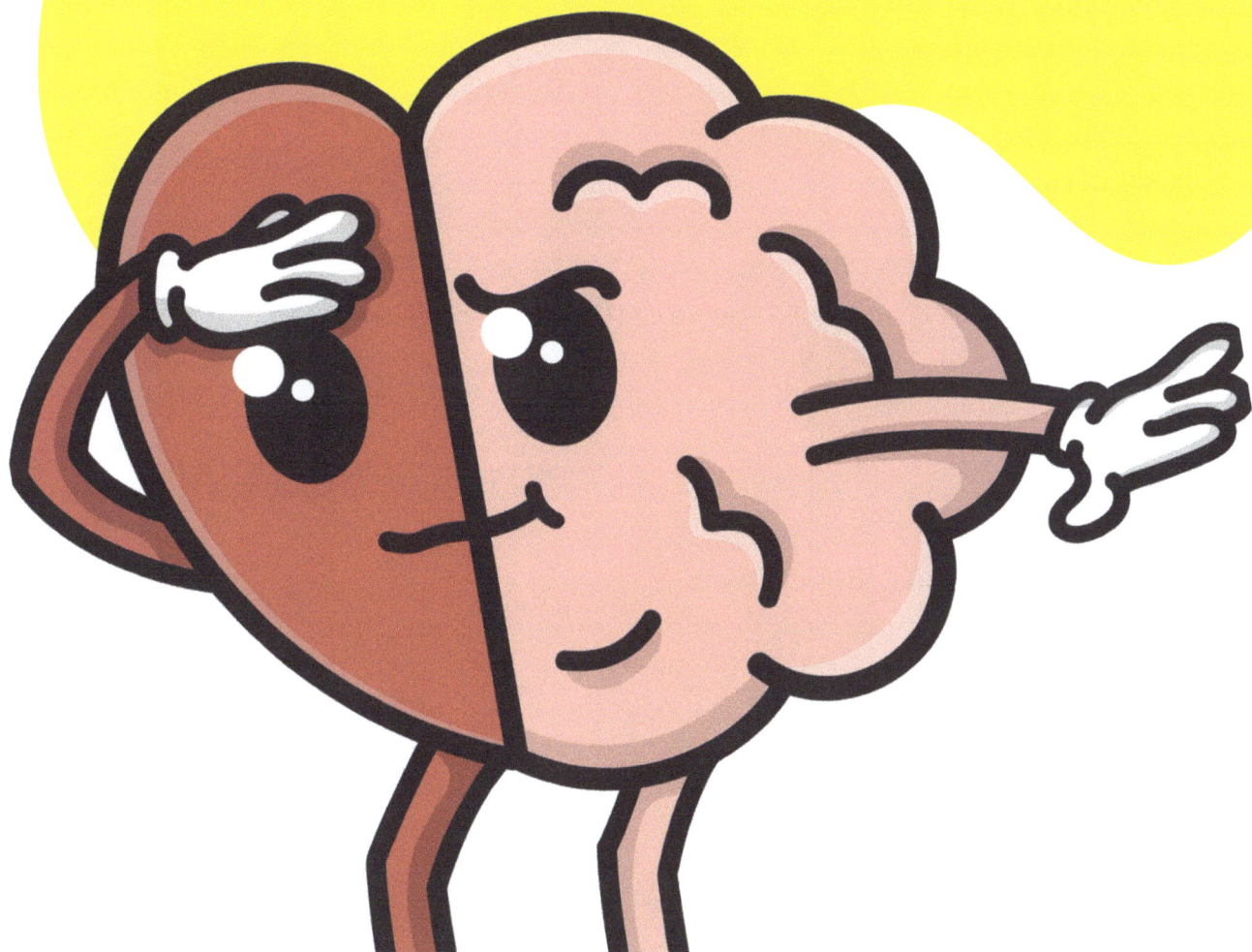

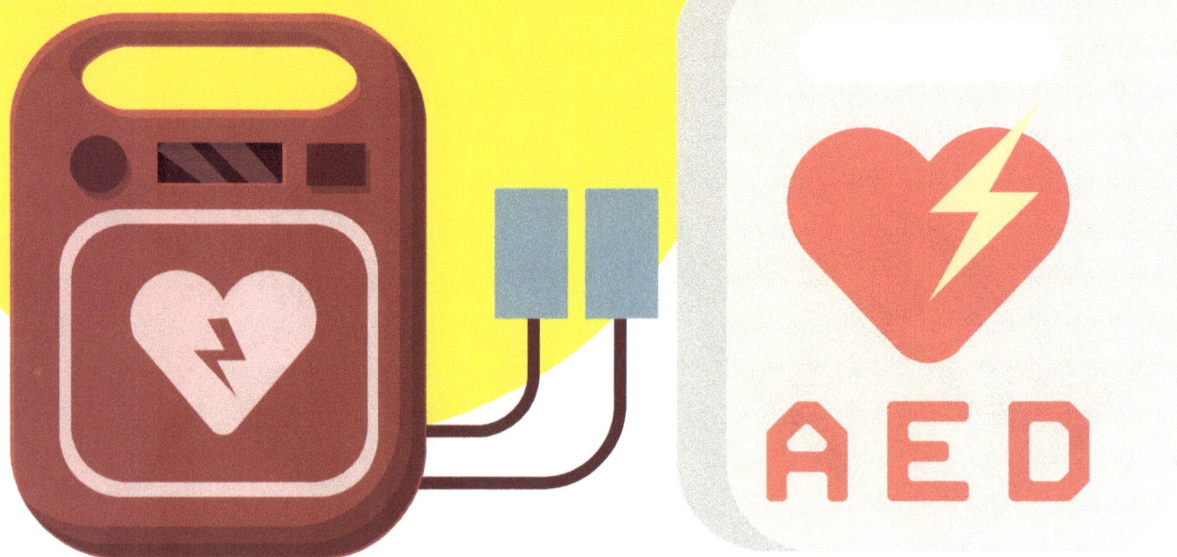

AEDs ARE MACHINES THAT OUR HEARTS USE AS TOOLS.

KEEP IT SIMPLE AND FOLLOW ALL STEPS BECAUSE THERE ARE SOME RULES.

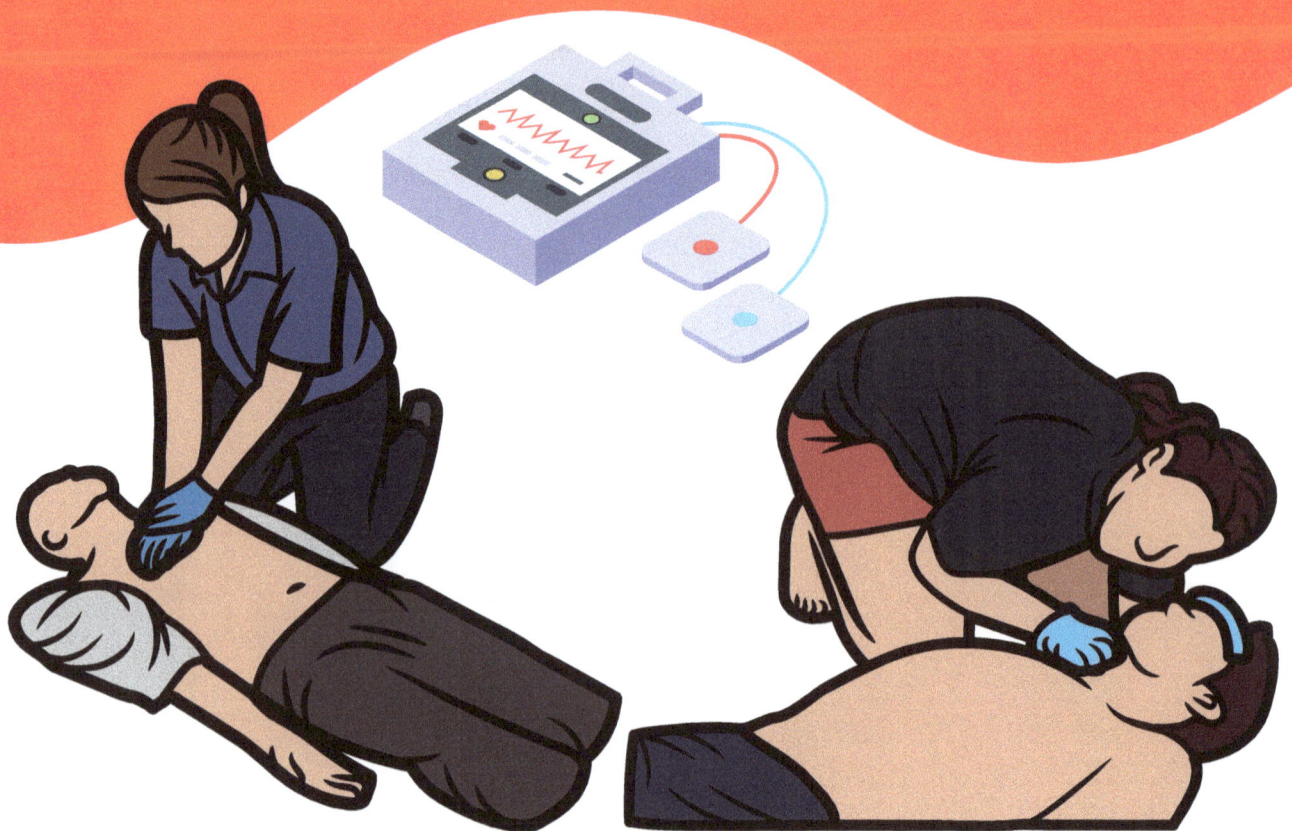

OPEN THE SHIRT, LOOK AT THE PICTURES, AND PLACE IT ON THE CHEST.

FOLLOW THE SIMPLE INSTRUCTIONS BECAUSE THIS MACHINE KNOWS BEST.

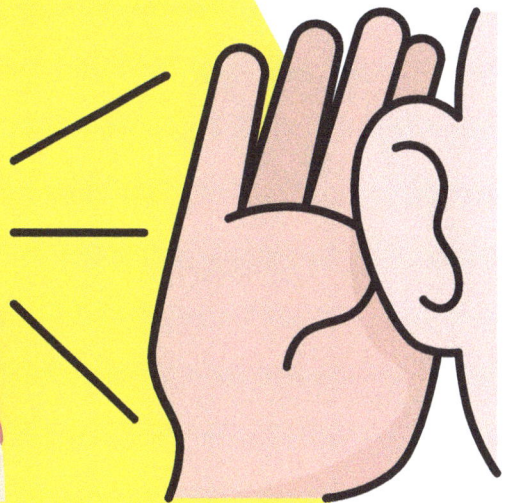

DANGER! DANGER! DANGER! DANGER! WE ARE READY TO SHOCK.

IF YOU OR ANYONE ELSE IS TOUCHING THIS PERSON, YOU'LL BE KNOCKED OFF YOUR SOCKS.

BOOM! BOOM!
ZAPP! ZAPP!
BUT THE JOB IS
STILL NOT DONE.

BACK ON THE CHEST FOR 5 CYCLES OF 30 AND 2.

NO MORE MOUTH TO MOUTH, JUST GOOD DEEP COMPRESSIONS WILL DO.

AND AS WE WAIT FOR THE FAST AMBULANCE TO ARRIVE.

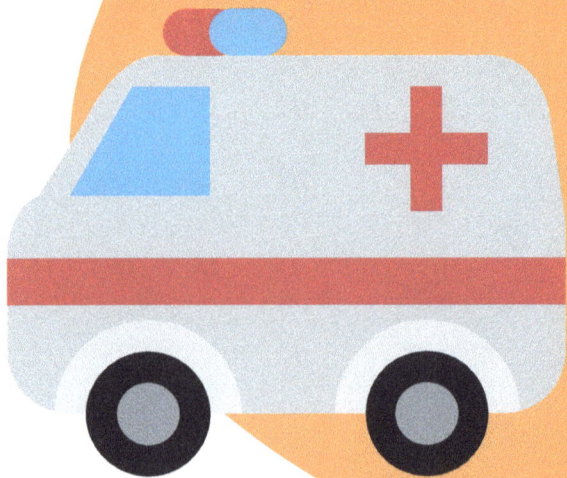

WE CAN FEEL GOOD AND PAT OUR BACKS THAT WE MIGHT HAVE HELPED SOMEONE SURVIVE.

SO THINK BACK TO THE BEGINNING OF THIS STORY OF WHAT YOU ALREADY KNEW.

SO PROUD OF YOU

YOU CAN DO IT

BELIEVE

YOURSELF!

KEEP

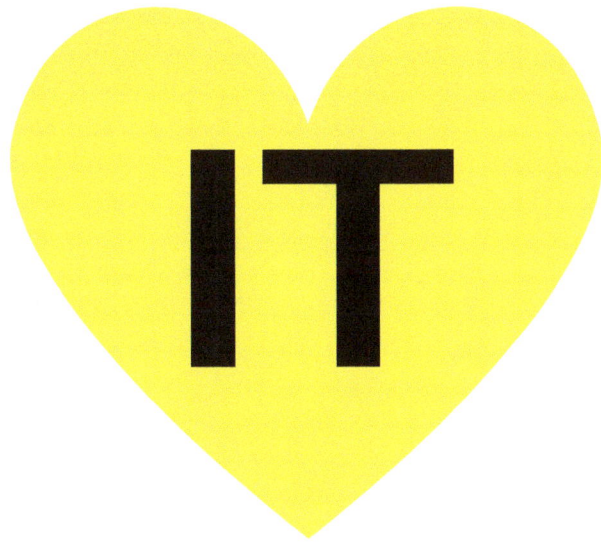

GOING!